# Squanto

## A STORY OF COMPASSION

*Written and Illustrated by*
*MarJean S. Peters*

*Artwriter Publishing*

Spokane, Washington

*Dedicated to*

*my precious seventeen grandchildren*

# Acknowledgements

THE CREDIT for this children's series goes to one inspirational woman. Vashti Young's passion and vision to teach and illustrate character qualities as tools for life gave me the incentive to write these stories and paint these pictures. She commission me in 2003 to supplement her curriculum called, *Tools For Life*, with stories and illustrations of real people in history who exemplified the character qualities she wanted to portray in her classes.

Her inspiration and insight spurred me on to write and create beyond my own imagination. God used her entrepreneurial passions to move me to work hard for many months at my easel to create these illustrations and stories. We stretched beyond our grasp in this faith venture and although *Tools For Life* did not hit the world market, it will continue to make a difference in people's lives through these books and Vashti's continued faithfulness to her vision.

# Table of Contents

# Compassion

**S**QUANTO knew how much it hurt to be mistreated. He knew how fear and loneliness felt. He knew the pain of disrespect from others, yet he chose not to treat others the way they handled him. Instead, he decided to show them compassion, which helped to heal his hurts and the hurts of others.

*COMPASSION willingly shares the feelings of someone else. All the jobs we do in life affect someone else: the way we get up in the morning; the way we act in school; the way we have fun. Compassion learns the boundaries of people around us and the places in their lives that hurt so we can protect those areas. Everything we do in life becomes harder when the people around us feel pain inside or out. Compassion allows us to understand these people, see things their way, and respect their boundaries.*

*—Vashti Young*

CHAPTER 1 CAPTURED

TISQUANTUM saw what looked like enormous white wings float into the bay above a giant canoe. As it neared his Patuxet Indian village, he and his friends crouched on the shore of the Great Waters to watch. Men let down smaller boats over the side of the ship by ropes and paddled them to shore. They wore unusual clothing, and hair nearly covered their white faces. They shouted strange words to one another and pointed to the wide-eyed Indian boys who lined the beach.

These men came on an English trading ship with Captain George Weymouth. They brought shiny beads and knives from the world across the Great Water to trade for furs and skins. At first, the sailors treated the boys well and even gave them some clothes to wear. They cunningly gained the boy's trust with their big smiles, colorful trinkets, and gifts.

When they prepared to leave, they motioned for the young braves to take a ride in their longboats. Many of the boys eagerly climbed aboard the longboats for a new adventure. As they pushed off from shore, Squanto's mother ran along the shore, "No! No!" She cried after them, "Tisquantum, come back! Come back!"

The longboats moved quickly along the surface of the water toward the great ship. The boys scrambled nimbly up the ropes that hung down the side of the boat, eager to explore this amazing vessel. As Squanto hoisted himself over the edge of the ship, two sailors suddenly grabbed him and threw him onto the deck. He gasped to catch his breath while coarse ropes cut into his wrists and ankles. The men hollered as they pulled their captors across the deck and dropped them into the dark belly of the ship. The boys' screams grew silent as the wind caught the sails, and the great ship began to move. Days, then weeks passed. Fear, loneliness, and seasickness seemed endless.

After three months at sea, the ship finally came to rest. Squanto had become accustomed to the darkness in the belly of the vessel. When the sailors pulled him out of the hold and led him down the gangplank, he tried to shield his eyes from the sudden and painful brightness of a strange world. When he finally looked up, he saw many huge buildings and crowds of people. He heard the sound of horses and carts clattering loudly over stone pathways. The scent of white men, fish, and smoke filled his nostrils. He shivered. What strange adventures awaited him in a world of people he could not trust.

## Chapter 2  SLAVE TRADERS

**T**HE SHIP finally reached the other side of the Atlantic Ocean, and the sailors took Squanto and the other Indians to the grand mansion of Sir Ferdinando Gorges. This man paid for the voyage and wanted these captured Indians to learn English to guide explorations into the New World. They sent Squanto to live with a man named Charles Robbins where he worked as a stable hand while he learned the English language.

Voyages to the New World cost a lot of money, and not many of them set out across the Atlantic. Several years passed and Squanto felt more and more homesick. Charles Robbins did his best to find a way for him to return to America. Finally, Robbins contacted Captain John Smith who planned a voyage to the New World. Smith agreed to take Squanto along if he worked as an interpreter for him after they reached America.

The captain finally gave Squanto permission to go home in 1614. How eager and excited he felt. Nearly ten years had passed since he last saw his family or his village. As he made his way home along the rocky coastline, he came across a group of European men camped along the shore. Squanto fearlessly talked with them in English.

Captain Thomas Hunt lead the group and showed friendliness to Squanto. When he told Squanto he wanted to show him his ship, Squanto trustingly followed the Captain. The minute he came on board, he knew he made another mistake. Once again the sailors imprisoned him. Once again they threw him into the hold of the ship where another twenty other Indians already sat in bondage.

This time the voyage grew even worse than before. Unrelenting storms lifted the waves high into the air, then dropped the ship into deep troughs between the waves. The prisoners often lost the little food given to them to seasickness or to the rats that watched for their scarce provisions. Weeks passed and some of the prisoners died. The sailors threw their bodies overboard and the ship continued on to Malaga, Spain.

When they finally sailed into port, the sailors pulled these miserably weak and sick survivors out of the hold, tied them together, and led them down a gangplank. One at a time they pushed them up on a high platform near the dock to sell them as slaves.

## Chapter 3   THE HOODED FIGURE

SQUANTO SWAYED weakly on the high platform in the Spanish slave port of Malaga. Foreign words echoed in his ears as the auctioneer shouted over the noise of the crowd.

Dust rose into the stifling air and stuck to the near naked bodies of the bronze-skinned prisoners. Squanto hung his head and closed his eyes and ears to the strangeness around him. He thought of his little village of bark-covered longhouses, of his tribe and family across that great tossing sea. He tried to remember the waving fields of corn, and the autumn woodlands ablaze with color where he used to hunt deer, wild turkeys, and flush up game hens for a feast.

The slave trader continued to shout. Squanto felt too sick to notice the hooded figure nearby until he stepped forward and emptied a leather pouch of coins into the trader's hand. Suddenly the hooded one reached out, took his arm, and led him down the steps. Squanto followed him through the crowded streets.

They came to the edge of the city and followed a narrow path that led to a large white house. When they entered the house, the man pulled back his hood to reveal a kind face and a broad smile. He carefully untied the slave's bleeding and ankles and wrists, then bandaged his wounds. "Estas libre!" he said, which meant, "You are free!" Other men, also dressed in brown robes, brought Squanto fresh water and good food, though he felt too sick to eat much.

Over the next few months, Squanto learned these men were monks. They called their big house a monastery where they lived to seek and serve God. As they nursed Squanto back to health, he came to understand why they showed him compassion. They believed God's Son, Jesus, bought their freedom out of compassion for them.

Years went by. Squanto learned their language, their customs, and more about their faith. After a day's work, he often sat on the balcony that overlooked the Great Sea. His heart longed for his home and family. His eyes scanned the deep blue and his heart yearned for his little village. He imagined his mother making cornbread, and gathering shellfish, and his father tending the fields or sharpening arrows. He saw his little brothers and sisters playing in the fields and eating berries in the woods while he ran with the young braves and threw his line to catch red herring.

## CHAPTER 4  HOMECOMING

THE SUN dipped below the sea while the sky reflected the last of its glory. Squanto had grown to become a man since he left his village. Though he cared deeply for the kind and compassionate monks, his heart ached for home.

Another morning came with the daily sound of bells and a hearty breakfast with his friends. But this morning was different. The monks told him they found passage for him on a fishing boat sailing from Spain to England. Squanto's quiet face brightened with hope and joy. When the day came to say goodbye, his heart felt heavy for he knew he would not see these friends again.

He sailed for England and found employment as a servant in the home of John Slanie, a London merchant. Slanie listened to Squanto's story and felt bad for him, but he was not eager for him to leave, nor was it easy to find passage to the New World. Three more years passed before Slanie found passage for Squanto. He finally crossed the Atlantic ocean for the fourth and last time in 1619. Again he worked as an interpreter for the ship's captain. Then one day Capt. Thomas Dermer called him into his cabin. What Squanto heard made his heart beat as hard as a ceremonial drum.

"Squanto, you served me well, and I release you to return to your people. You may go now," he said. Squanto wasted no time and soon sprinted along the rocky shore.

A thousand happy pictures filled his mind as he neared his village and a thousand questions. Would they recognize the man he had become? He bounded over the rocky terrain, but his steps slowed as an eerie silence greeted him. No dogs barked, no children's voices, and no faces greeted him. The longhouses stood dark and empty, and grass covered the old pathways. He moved through the abandoned village as if in a strange dream until he came to the graves on the other side. It neared nightfall when Squanto built a fire from the fallen wood and bark. He sat quietly alone before the fire as sparks rose into the darkness.

At sunrise, he walked to the neighboring Wampanoag village. They told him a "great sickness" struck his people. Squanto was the last of his tribe. With no home or people, he ran into the forest. Weeks went by while he wandered through the forest in his

grief. Images of his people and the strange events of his life filled his heart and mind. What would he do? Where could he go? In his loneliness, Squanto slowly found his way back to the Indian village of Wampanoag.

## CHAPTER 5  COMPASSION

CHIEF MASSASOIT allowed Squanto to live in his village and Squanto tried hard to settle into the Wampanoag tribe. Then one day his friend, Samoset, returned from a hunting trip and told them about a group of white settlers building a town where Squanto's tribe used to live. Because Squanto taught Samoset some of the English language, he learned that many of the immigrants died from the cold and lack of food the winter before. When Samoset asked Squanto to go back with him to help them, Squanto needed to make an important decision.

White men had tricked and captured him twice. They took him from his people. Some treated him harshly and tried to sell him in the slave market. Now white men used the land where his people once lived and died. How could he trust them? Why should he help them?

The kind face of the hooded figure who purchased his freedom suddenly loomed into Squanto's mind. He thought of the stories the monks told him and why they set him free. Squanto looked into the sky that covered the whole earth. He looked out at the Great Waters that connected the White Man and the Indian. He looked at the forests, the streams, and hills around him and then he thought of the Settlers. Many of them already died because they did not know how to survive in this land. They needed someone to teach them how to build warm houses, plant food, fish, and hunt. Suddenly Squanto's heart filled with compassion.

He joined Chief Massasoit in a meeting with the Settlers on March 22, 1621. The Indians and Settlers talked and listened as Squanto interpreted between them. The Settlers called themselves Pilgrims. They used to live in England, but because they worshipped

God differently, the English people arrested them and threw them into jail. They left England to live in Holland. In time they faced the same the same thing in Holland. From there they crossed the ocean to raise their children in the freedom of the New World. They called their settlement New Plymouth, in honor of the town in England where they once lived.

Through Squanto's interpretation and mediation, he helped the Indians and Pilgrims understand one another and work out an agreement that allowed the two groups to live peacefully. That day Massasoit and the colonial governor, William Bradford, signed the first diplomatic treaty in North America, an agreement of peace and mutual protection. This peace treaty lasted for over fifty years.

## CHAPTER 6    THANKSGIVING

THE DELEGATION of Indians turned to leave New Plymouth and Squanto turned his face toward the small group of Pilgrims. He noticed the trees were ready to bud, and these people did not know how to plant corn, or catch enough fish, or hunt enough animals to survive another winter. He knew he could not leave them.

Spring brought a new beginning. The Pilgrims trusted and gladly welcomed Squanto. A few weeks later tree branches formed buds, and Squanto told the

Pilgrims it was time to plant corn. He taught them how to catch red herring for food and how to plant fish in each hill of corn for fertilizer. Spring grew into summer while they fished and collected shellfish. The sun beat down, the corn ripened, and Squanto helped the Pilgrims harvest the big yellow cobs. He also showed the women how to cook the corn.

When Autumn came, they gathered wild fruit, onions, potatoes, and hunted game. They harvested maize, beans, and pumpkins. Dried venison hung from the ceilings and fish dried on racks, ready to store for the winter. Squanto helped the Pilgrims get along with the nearby Indian tribes. He interpreted for them, guided them on trading expeditions, and gave advice on trading.

The driving snows of winter arrived, but Squanto and the Pilgrims remained snug and dry in the warm houses he helped them build. When spring returned, they still had enough seeds for spring planting. They also had enough food to carry them through until they harvested the next crop.

For eighteen months, Squanto remained with the Pilgrims. When autumn arrived again, the Pilgrims planned a feast to celebrate God's merciful help. They sent Squanto to invite Chief Massasoit and his braves.

The Pilgrims and ninety braves feasted for days on venison, roast duck and goose, turkeys, shellfish, bread, vegetables, and woodland berries.

Before they feasted, the Pilgrim men removed their wide-brimmed hats, and the Indians stood reverently as the Pilgrim governor, William Bradford, led them in a prayer of thanksgiving. He thanked God for all He provided. He thanked God for Squanto whom God prepared and sent to show them how to live in this new land.

Squanto looked out over the tables full of food. He looked at the Pilgrims and Indians feasting together. He gazed out over the Great Waters. He thought of the hooded figure who bought him and set him free, of the monks who treated him so kindly and shared their faith with him. He would not forget them and his heart filled with thanksgiving.

## CHAPTER 7  A STRONG PERSON

A GLORIOUS Indian summer in late October of 1622 blazed the hills with red and gold. Autumn breezes stirred the heart to adventure. When William Bradford invited Squanto to join him on an expedition around Cape Cod, Squanto eagerly went. He and the Pilgrims had already gathered in the harvest, stored the fish and venison, and made everything ready for another winter.

Only a week or so into the journey around the Cape, Squanto held his head in pain. By nightfall, he shivered uncontrollably. His fever persisted for several days causing the expedition to come to a halt. By the time little bumps appeared on his hands and face, Squanto knew that the Great Sickness in his tribe found him as well.

The cold chill of that starlit night could not cool Squanto's body. William Bradford knelt at his bedside. "Pray for me, Governor," the Indian whispered, "that I might go to the Englishmen's God in heaven." Bradford prayed, and Squanto took his last breath.

William Bradford picked up his pen, opened his inkwell, and in the lantern light wrote in his diary, "... Squanto became a special instrument sent of God for good..., he showed how to plant corn, where to take fish and to procure other commodities. He was also pilot to bring us to unknown places for profit, and never left us till he died."

That was almost 400 years ago. Today we still want to remember Squanto. We want to recognize him because he used the hard things in his life to make him more compassionate toward people who were hurting. Squanto knew the pain of mistreatment by others. He knew fear and loneliness. He knew how much it cut when others disrespected him. He could choose to become very bitter and mean to other people because of their meanness to him. Even when his entire tribe died and all seemed lost, God's purpose began to unfold. Squanto decided on another way to heal his hurts and the hurts of others. He chose to remember the compassion shown to him by the monks instead of the English and slave traders' injustice. He chose to show compassion to the Mayflower pilgrims, which saved them from starvation.

With the highest price in the universe, our Creator paid to buy us out of another kind of slave market. He also set us free for a higher purpose. He loves us and becomes our place to run and find peace and joy. Often what seems like a complete loss becomes a stepping stone to God's higher purpose. We cannot understand everything that happens in our lives but we choose to believe in the One who gave His life-blood for us and lives again.

Always remember that real strength has nothing to do with the size of our muscles. Power to love others comes from God who forgives and pours His strength into us. Who is strong enough to show compassion to someone who hurts them? It takes a mighty person do that. The strongest people in the world show compassion.

# About the Author

MarJean and her husband of nearly fifty years live in Spokane, Washington. Their four children gave them seventeen amazing grandchildren. When their own children were still little, their daddy told them "Chippy" stories on many nights before bed. The family of chipmunks went on many crazy, fun-filled adventures that always taught them some of life-lesson.

After their four children grew up, the stories continued for the grandchildren who begged for a Chippy story whenever Papa and Gramma visited and stayed over-night. The grandchildren got so into the stories that they kept making suggestions for the outcome, which Papa quickly incorporated into his seat-of-the-pants tall tales.

Gramma's gifts never fell into Papa's extroverted, smooth talking, Tom-foolery yarns that kept the children in stitches. Perhaps someday those stories will find themselves into books, but until then Gramma uses her artistic talents to bring to you other adventures based on real-life people who still teach us essential values.

Besides their family, MarJean and Conrad enjoy their two adorable Havanese pups, Smoky and Snickers—velcro dogs that never leave their sides, as well as their very noisy and sometimes obnoxious parakeets named Cheerio and Fruit Loop.

Their adventurous lives span the Pacific Northwest, California, Canada, and Alaska, which gives them a rich variety of culture, friends, and experiences out of which to tell you stories.

Made in the USA
Coppell, TX
07 April 2022

76168115R00024